# Interactive Daily
# TEKS/TAKS Review
## Workbook

**Grade 1**

Scott Foresman · Addison Wesley

# enVisionMATH™
# Texas

**Editorial Offices:** Glenview, Illinois · Parsippany, New Jersey · New York, New York
**Sales Offices:** Boston, Massachusetts · Duluth, Georgia · Glenview, Illinois
Coppell, Texas · Sacramento, California · Mesa, Arizona

ISBN – 13: 978-0-328-34367-6

ISBN – 10: 0-328-34367-6

enVisionMATH Texas is trademarked in the U.S. and/or foreign countries of Pearson Education, Inc. or its affiliate(s).

5  6  7  8  9  10  V004  12  11

**1.** How many more dogs than bones?

○ 1 more

● 2 more

○ 3 more

○ 4 more

**2.** Which piece of toast is cut into halves?

○ A

○ B

○ C

● D

A     B

C     D

**3.** Circle the object that is below the teddy bear.

Name_____

**1.** Count the flowers.
Tell how many.

- ⬭ 2
- ⬭ 3
- ▬ 4
- ⬭ 5

**2.** Which shows the number 3?

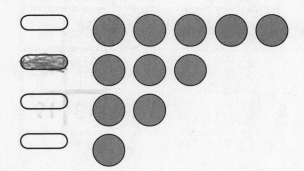

**3.** Circle the child who is second
in line.

Name_____

1. Maritza drew this pattern.
   Which shapes come next?

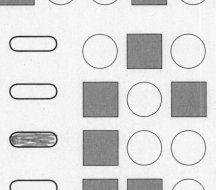

2. What day of the week
   is July 10?

   ⬭  Thursday

   ⬭  Friday

   ⬭  Saturday

   ⬭  Sunday

| JULY | | | | | | |
|---|---|---|---|---|---|---|
| **S** | **M** | **T** | **W** | **T** | **F** | **S** |
| | | 1 | 2 | 3 | 4 | 5 |
| 6 | 7 | 8 | 9 | 10 | 11 | 12 |
| 13 | 14 | 15 | 16 | 17 | 18 | 19 |

3. Kim counted the ants.
   Write the number that
   tells how many.

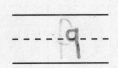

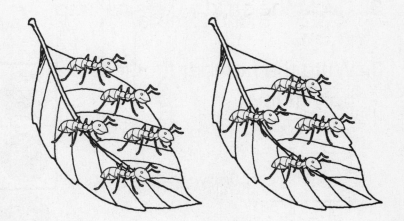

3

**1.** Mandy ate 3 crackers.
Then she ate 3 more.
Which shows how many
crackers Mandy ate?

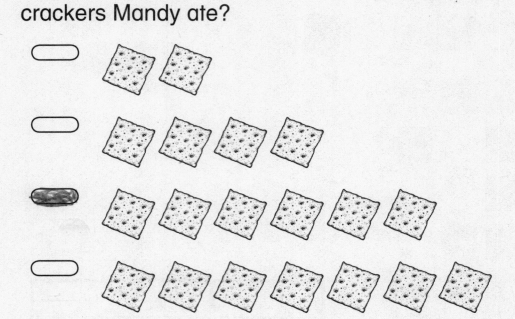

**2.** 9 is 8 and 1 more.
What is 10?

◯  7 and 1 more

◯  7 and 2 more

⬤  8 and 1 less

◯  8 and 2 more

**3.** Write the number that tells
how many.

**1.** Dana drew this dot pattern.
What number does Dana's
pattern show?

- ⬭ 9
- ⬬ 8
- ⬭ 7
- ⬭ 6

**2.** Which does the ten-frame show?

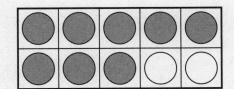

- ⬬ 8 and 1 more
- ⬭ 8 and 2 more
- ⬭ 8 and 1 less
- ⬭ 8 and 2 less

**3.** Draw the dot pattern that comes next.

**1.** Eli makes a pattern with buttons.
How many buttons does he use?

- 9
- 8
- 6
- 3

**2.** Which number tells how many?

- 5
- 6
- 7
- 8

**3.** Draw the missing dots to make 9 in all.

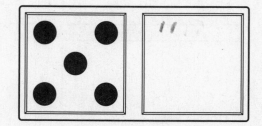

**1.** Which number tells how many?

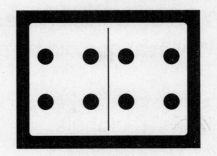

 4

 6

 8

 10

**2.** How many more counters do you need to make 12?

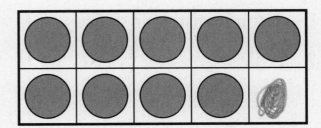

 1

 2

 3

 4

**3.** Draw the next shape in the pattern.

△ ◯ △ ◯ △ ◯ △ ◯ △

1. Tom drew this shape.
   Which shape did he draw?

   ⬭ circle
   ⬛ rectangle
   ⬭ square
   ⬭ triangle

2. Ken had 4 toy cars.
   Lakin gave him 4 more.
   Which number shows
   how many cars Ken has now?

   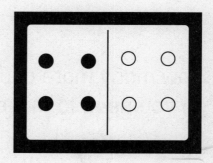

   ⬭ 4
   ⬭ 6
   ⬛ 8
   ⬭ 10

3. Write the numbers.
   Circle **is less than** or **is greater than**.

   _6_   is less than   _P_
         is greater than

1. Phil caught 8 butterflies.
   Now he has 11 butterflies.
   How many more butterflies
   did Phil catch?

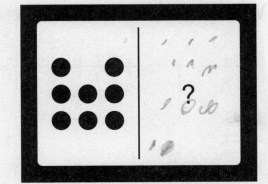

    19
   ⬭ 11
   ⬭ 4
   ⬭ 3

2. Jane is first in line.
   Who is fourth in line?

   ⬭ Jane
   ⬭ Liz
   ⬭ May
    Sam

   Jane    Liz    May    Sam

3. Andy eats 6 grapes.
   Marla eats 3 grapes.
   Ellie eats 8 grapes.
   Put these numbers in order
   from least to greatest.

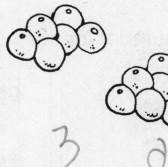

   3         2         8
   ___      ___      ___
   least   between   greatest

e_____

Which number is before 8 and after 6?

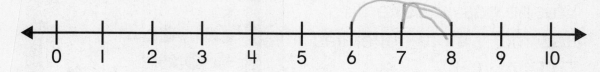

| 0 | 1 | 2 | 3 | 4 | 5 | 6 | 7 | 8 | 9 | 10 |

- ⬭ 9
- ⬭ 8
- ⬭ 7
- ⬭ 6

2. Alice has 6 pencils.
Bill has 4 pencils.
Doug has 1 fewer
pencil than Bill.

Which shows the numbers in
order from greatest to least?

- ⬭ 6, 4, 3
- ⬭ 4, 6, 3
- ⬭ 3, 6, 4
- ⬭ 3, 4, 6

3. Write the number for each dot pattern.

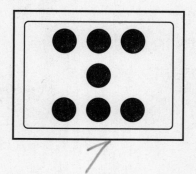

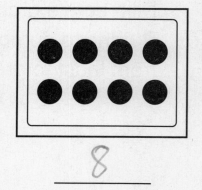

____6____          ____7____          ____8____

Name_____

**1.** How many toy cars is
1 less than 6 cars?

　　⬭　　4 cars

　　⬭　　5 cars

　　⬭　　6 cars

　　⬭　　7 cars

**2.** Which number is greater than 8
and less than 11?

　　⬭　　13

　　⬭　　9

　　⬭　　7

　　⬭　　6

**3.** Write the number that tells
how many in all.

**1.** Which shows the numbers in order
from least to greatest?

    ⬭    8, 5, 1

    ⬭    1, 8, 5

    ⬭    5, 1, 8

    ⬭    1, 5, 8

**2.** Which tells how many in all?

    ⬭    0

    ⬭    3

    ⬭    6

    ⬭    7

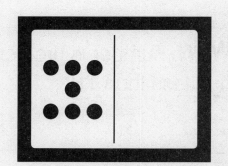

**3.** Write the number inside and outside.
Then write the number in all.

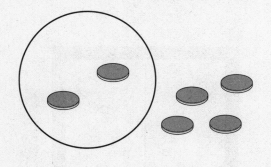

    2      4      6

  inside   outside   in all

**1.** 8 is 7 and 1 more.
What is 9?

⬭ 7 and 3 more

⬭ 7 and 2 more

⬭ 7 and 1 more

⬭ 6 and 2 more

**2.** Tania has the shortest pencil.
Which pencil does Tania have?

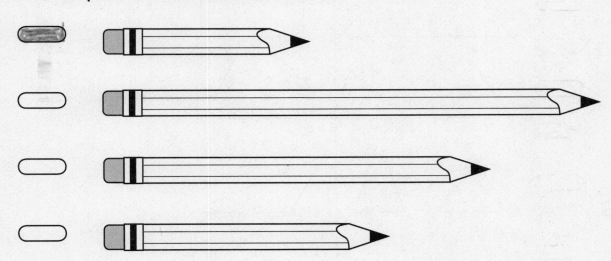

**3.** Draw the missing dots
so there are 8 dots in all.
Then write the number
of missing dots.

8
_____

**1.** Which is the same as 2 and 7?

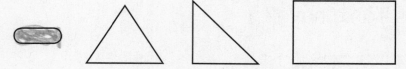     1 and 1

    2 and 5

    3 and 4

    4 and 5

**2.** Craig drew 2 triangles and 1 rectangle.
Which shapes did Craig draw?

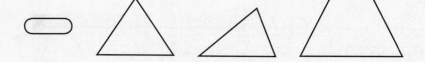

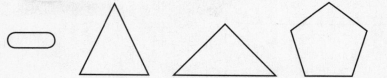

**3.** Draw the missing dot pattern.

**1.** Which number does the picture show?

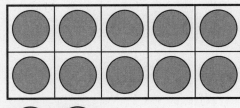

 12

◯ 11

◯ 10

◯ 2

**2.** Marni drew some flowers. Which addition sentence goes with Marni's picture?

◯  6 + 1 = 7

⬭  6 + 2 = 8

◯  7 + 2 = 9

◯  7 + 3 = 10

**3.** Write the missing numbers.

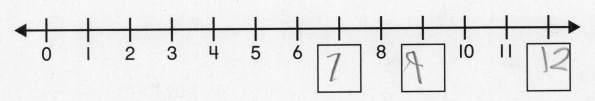

0  1  2  3  4  5  6  ⬚7  8  ⬚9  10  11  ⬚12

1. Brett and Greg collect baseball hats.
   Brett has 6 hats.
   Greg has 3 hats.
   Which addition sentence shows
   how many hats in all?

   ⬭  3 + 3 = 6
   ⬭  6 + 0 = 6
   ⬭  6 + 3 = 9
   ⬭  6 + 6 = 12

2. Which shape comes next in the pattern?

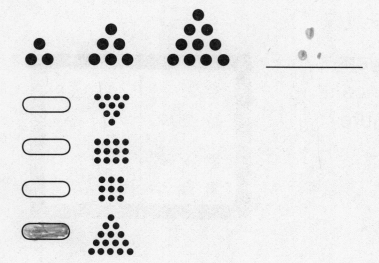

3. Write each number.
   Then circle **is less than**
   or **is greater than**.

   ___6___   is less than   ___8___
             is greater than

**1.** Ellen has a bag of 6 apples.
Donna has a bag of 4 apples.

Which addition sentence shows
how many apples in all?

   ⬭      $6 + 6 = 12$

   ⬮      $6 + 4 = 10$

   ⬭      $6 + 3 = 9$

   ⬭      $4 + 4 = 8$

**2.** Which numbers are between 5 and 9?

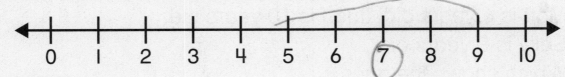

   ⬭      2, 3, 4

   ⬭      9, 10, 11

   ⬮      6, 7, 8

   ⬭      3, 5, 9

**3.** Draw the missing dot pattern.

1. Jack saw 7 ducks in the pond.
   Hanna saw more ducks than Jack.
   Which is more than 7?

    ⬭    3 ducks

    ⬭    5 ducks

    ⬭    7 ducks

    ⬭    9 ducks

2. Matt is 6 years old. Juan is 10 years old.
   Sally is 8 years old.
   Which shows the ages
   from least to greatest?

    ⬭    10, 8, 6

    ⬭    10, 6, 8

    ⬭    8, 6, 10

    ⬭    6, 8, 10

3. Write a number sentence that
   tells how many dots in all.

    3 + 4 = 7

    ___ + ___ = ___

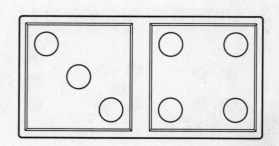

Name_____

1. There are 6 pieces of fruit.
   4 of them are oranges.
   The rest are bananas.
   How many bananas are there?

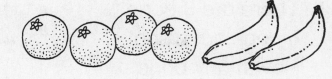

   - ⬭ 1
   - ⬭ 2
   - ⬭ 3
   - ⬭ 4

2. Kenny scores 3 goals
   in the soccer game.
   Then Kenny scores 2 more goals.
   How many goals did Kenny
   score in all?

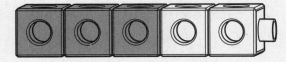

   - ⬭ 7
   - ⬭ 6
   - ⬭ 5
   - ⬭ 1

3. Draw a different dot pattern
   that shows 6.

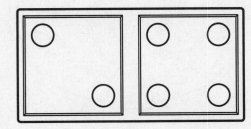   

Name_____

**1.** There are 8 dogs.
6 dogs have spots.
How many dogs
have no spots?

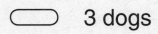 2 dogs

◯ 3 dogs

◯ 4 dogs

◯ 5 dogs

**2.** Becky has 7 pencils.
David has 3 pencils.
How many pencils are
there in all?

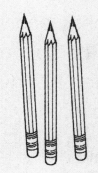

◯ 11

◼ 10

◯ 5

◯ 4

**3.** There are fish in a fishbowl.
2 are large fish.
5 are small.

Write two different number
sentences about the fish.

___2___ + ___7___ = ___7___

___2___ + ___2___ = ___7___

20

1. There are 9 glasses.
   7 glasses are on the table.
   The other glasses are in the sink.
   How many glasses are in the sink?

   ⬭ 6

   ⬭ 4

   ⬭ 3

   ⬬ 2

2. Today is Sarah's birthday.
   Sarah is between 9 and 11 years old.
   How old is Sarah?

   ⬭ 6 years old

   ⬭ 8 years old

   ⬬ 10 years old

   ⬭ 12 years old

3. Draw a picture to solve.
   Carol has 3 black marbles.
   She has 4 white marbles.
   How many marbles does
   Carol have in all?

   _7___ marbles

1. Marie has 7 marbles in a bag.
   She takes 4 out of the bag.
   Which number sentence tells
   how many marbles are
   in the bag now?

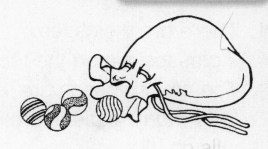

   ⬭  $7 - 1 = 6$

   ⬭  $4 - 3 = 1$

   ⬭  $7 - 3 = 4$

   ⬬  $7 - 4 = 3$

2. Debbie put 2 books in her bag.
   Then she added 3 books
   to her bag.
   How many books does
   Debbie have in all?

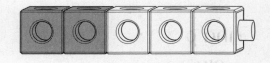

   ⬭  1

   ⬭  4

   ⬬  5

   ⬭  6

3. Write a number sentence that tells
   about the picture.

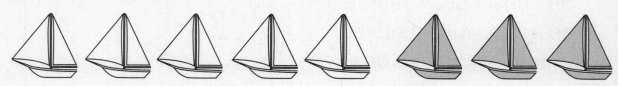

   __5__ + __3__ = __8__

Name_____

**1.** 7 ants are on a log.
2 ants run away.
How many ants are left?
Which subtraction sentence
tells about the story?

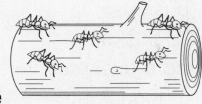

- $5 = 7 - 2$
- $2 = 7 - 5$
- $5 - 2 = 3$
- $7 - 5 = 2$

**2.** John plants 4 flowers in the garden.
Tina plants 5 flowers in the garden.
Which number sentence tells how
many flowers in all?

- $9 - 4 = 5$
- $9 - 5 = 4$
- $4 + 5 = 9$
- $5 + 9 = 14$

**3.** Circle numbers that are between 3 and 7.

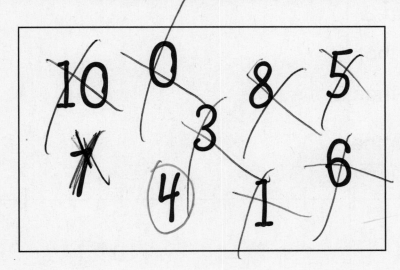

10    0    8    5
      3
   4    1    6

**1.** Al makes 6 baskets.
Jose makes 2 baskets.
How many more baskets
does Al make than Jose?

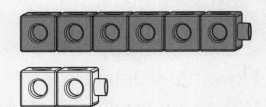

- ⬤ 2
- ◯ 3
- ◯ 4
- ◯ 8

**2.** There are 2 swans in the pond.
There are 5 ducks in the pond.
Which sentence tells about the story?

- ◯ 5 is less than 2.
- ◯ 2 is less than 2.
- ◯ 2 is greater than 5.
- ⬤ 5 is greater than 2.

**3.** Write the missing numbers.

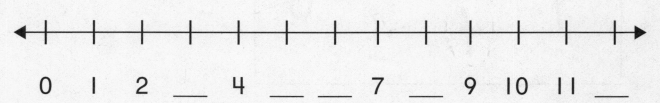

0   1   2   __   4   __   __   7   __   9   10   11   __

**1.** Rowena has 🍎🍎🍎🍎🍎🍎🍎🍎 .

Jon has 🍎🍎🍎🍎🍎🍎🍎🍎🍎🍎 .

Gil has 🍎🍎🍎🍎🍎🍎 .

Which shows the number of apples
in order from greatest to least?

⬭ 8, 6, 10

⬭ 6, 10, 8

⬭ 10, 8, 6

⬭ 10, 6, 8

**2.** Marcus has 4 hamsters.
Joan has 4 more hamsters than Marcus.
Which shows how many hamsters Joan has?

⬭ 6

⬭ 7

⬭ 8

⬭ 9

**3.** Marlo buys some fish.
She puts 5 fish in a large tank.
She puts 3 fish in a fish bowl.

Write an addition sentence to
show how many fish in all.

_____ + _____ = _____

**1.** Which number tells
how many cats in all?

- ⬭ 9
- ⬭ 8
- ⬭ 5
- ⬭ 4

**2.** Miguel feeds 5 horses.
Betty feeds 3 horses.
How many more horses
does Miguel feed than Betty?

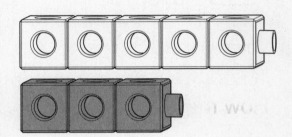

- ⬭ 2
- ⬭ 3
- ⬭ 4
- ⬭ 8

**3.** Write an addition sentence
that tells about the picture.
Then write a related
subtraction sentence.

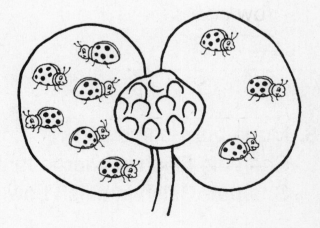

_____ + _____ = _____

_____ − _____ = _____

**1.** Nina had 8 dolls.
   She gave 3 to her sister.
   Which shows how many dolls Nina has left?

   ⬭  8 + 3 = 11

   ⬭  11 − 3 = 8

   ⬭  8 − 3 = 5

   ⬭  8 − 5 = 3

**2.** There are 5 books on the desk.
   There are 3 books on the floor.
   How many books are there in all?

   ⬭  2

   ⬭  7

   ⬭  8

   ⬭  9

**3.** Draw counters to show 7.

**1.** 3 lions are sleeping.
2 more join them.
Which shows how many lions in all?

- ⬭ 1 + 2 = 3
- ⬭ 2 + 2 = 4
- ⬭ 3 + 1 = 4
- ⬭ 3 + 2 = 5

**2.** Which number tells how many fish in all?

- ⬭ 8
- ⬭ 7
- ⬭ 3
- ⬭ 2

**3.** Write the missing numbers.

5 + _____ = _____

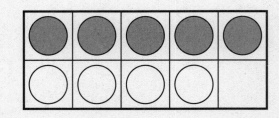

**1.** Which pattern does the number line show?

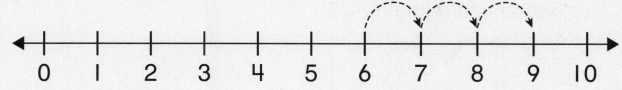

- ⬭ add 0
- ⬭ add 1
- ⬭ add 2
- ⬭ add 4

**2.** 6 take away 3 is _____.

- ⬭ 9
- ⬭ 6
- ⬭ 3
- ⬭ 0

**3.** Write the numbers in order from least to greatest.

_____   _____        _____
least                  greatest

**I.** Which addition sentence goes
with the picture Mia drew?

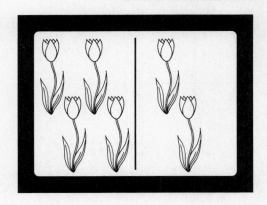

- ⬭  $4 + 4 = 8$
- ⬭  $4 + 2 = 6$
- ⬭  $2 + 3 = 5$
- ⬭  $1 + 4 = 5$

**2.** Jon's pencil measures about 3 clips long.
Nina's pencil measures 1 clip longer
than Jon's pencil.
About how long is Nina's pencil?

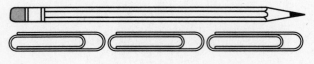

- ⬭  7 clips
- ⬭  6 clips
- ⬭  5 clips
- ⬮  4 clips

**3.** Write the numbers that show how to make 10.
Look for a pattern.

$10 + $ _____ $= 10$

$9 + $ _____ $= 10$

$8 + $ _____ $= 10$

**1.** Which two addition sentences
tell about the cubes?

- 6 + 2 = 8
  2 + 6 = 8

- 3 + 3 = 6
  4 + 4 = 8

- 6 + 2 = 8
  3 + 5 = 8

- 6 + 0 = 6
  2 + 0 = 2

**2.** Tony's shirt has 2 pockets.
He puts 6 pennies in each pocket.
Which tells how many pennies
Tony has in his pockets?

- 2 + 2 = 4

- 2 + 4 = 6

- 2 + 6 = 8

- 6 + 6 = 12

**3.** Circle the larger sum.

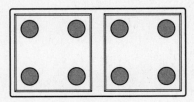    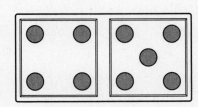

4 + 4        4 + 5

Name_____

1. The graph shows the number of peaches
   Nina and Kimi picked.

| Picked Peaches | | | | | | | | | | |
|---|---|---|---|---|---|---|---|---|---|---|
| Nina | | | | | | | | | | |
| Kimi | | | | | | | | | | |

0  1  2  3  4  5  6  7  8  9

Which number sentence tells how many peaches
Nina and Kimi picked in all?

⬭  $7 - 6 = 1$

⬭  $13 - 6 = 7$

⬭  $6 + 6 = 12$

⬭  $6 + 7 = 13$

2. Pete blows up 5 balloons.
   Juan blows up 1 more balloon
   than Pete.
   Which shows how many
   balloons Pete and Juan
   blow up in all?

⬭  $5 + 6 = 11$

⬭  $5 + 5 = 10$

⬭  $5 + 4 = 9$

⬭  $1 + 5 = 6$

3. Write what comes next.

$1 + 1 = 2$    $2 + 2 = 4$    $3 + 3 = 6$    ___ + ___ = ___

© Pearson Education, Inc. 1

Name_____

**1.** Which tells about the ten-frame?

⬭  3 + 0 = 3

⬭  5 + 0 = 5

⬭  5 + 3 = 8

⬭  8 + 3 = 11

**2.** Max's dodgeball team has 8 players.
2 more players sign up for his team.
Which addition fact shows how many
players Max's team has now?

⬭  8 + 0 = 8

⬭  8 + 2 = 10

⬭  10 + 2 = 12

⬭  8 + 8 = 16

**3.** Write an addition sentence for the picture.

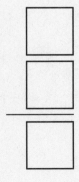 

**1.** Louis draws a pattern of dots.
Which number does his pattern show?

⬭  3

⬭  4

⬭  5

⬭  6

**2.** Harold has 7 movie tickets.
Lilly has 5 tickets.
How many movie tickets
do they have in all?

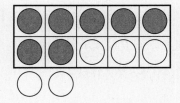

⬭  2

⬭  3

⬭  11

⬭  12

**3.** Write an addition sentence for the picture.

_____ + _____ = _____

**1.** Which addition sentence with 10 shows how many beach balls in all?

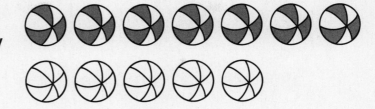

   ⬭   10 + 7 = 17

   ⬭   10 + 5 = 15

   ⬭   10 + 3 = 13

   ⬭   10 + 2 = 12

**2.** Count back to subtract.
Use the number line.

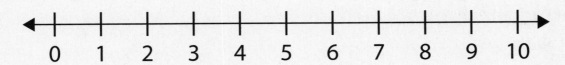

0  1  2  3  4  5  6  7  8  9  10

9 − 2 = _____

   ⬭   6

   ⬭   7

   ⬭   8

   ⬭   11

**3.** Write a double or near double fact for each sum.

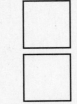 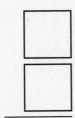  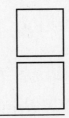

**1.** Find the missing number.

⬚ is more than 5 but less than 10.

⚬ 4

⚬ 5

⚬ 7

⚬ 12

**2.** Adam lost 1 crayon.
He only has 9 crayons now.
How many crayons did Adam
start with?

⚬ 11

⚬ 10

⚬ 9

⚬ 8

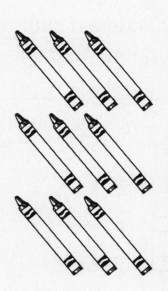

**3.** There are 2 benches in the park.
Kia sees 4 children sitting
on one bench.
She sees no children
on the other bench.

Write a number sentence to
show how many children Kia sees.

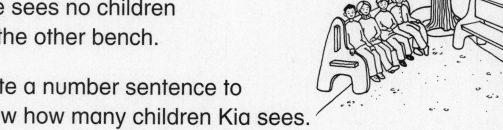

_____ + _____ = _____

**1.** Which related addition and subtraction sentences match the picture?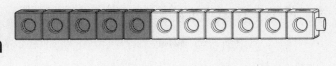

    ⬭   $5 + 6 = 11$
             $11 - 6 = 5$

    ⬭   $5 + 1 = 6$
             $6 - 1 = 5$

    ⬭   $5 + 1 = 6$
             $6 + 5 = 11$

    ⬭   $6 + 5 = 11$
             $5 + 6 = 11$

**2.** Which doubles fact helps you solve $10 - 5$?

    ⬭   $3 + 3 = 6$

    ⬭   $4 + 4 = 8$

    ⬭   $5 + 5 = 10$

    ⬭   $6 + 6 = 12$

**3.** The shelf in Danelle's room holds 9 books.
7 books are on the shelf.
How many books are missing?

Complete the addition and subtraction sentences to solve.

_____ + _____ = 9         $9 -$ _____ = _____

_____ books

Name_____

**1.** Which related facts match
the picture?

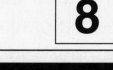

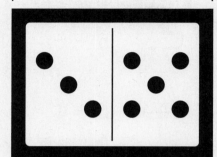

  ⬭     3 + 3 = 6
        10 − 5 = 5

  ⬭     3 + 5 = 8
        8 − 3 = 5

  ⬭     8 + 3 = 11
        11 − 3 = 8

  ⬭     8 + 3 = 11
        5 + 6 = 11

**2.** Tia had 6 crackers.
She ate 5 of those crackers.
Which addition fact will help you find
how many crackers Tia has left?

  ⬭     5 + 0 = 5

  ⬭     6 + 0 = 6

  ⬭     5 + 1 = 6

  ⬭     6 + 5 = 11

**3.** Write a subtraction sentence.
Then write how many fewer dogs.

____ ◯ ____ ◯ ____

_____ fewer dogs

**1.** The plant has 12 flowers.
5 flowers are picked.
Which addition fact shows how many flowers are left?

    ⬭   $5 + 5 = 10$

    ⬭   $8 + 4 = 12$

    ⬭   $5 + 7 = 12$

    ⬭   $12 + 5 = 17$

**2.** Carlos sees 2 rabbits.
Tina sees 7 rabbits.
Which shows how many
rabbits they see in all?

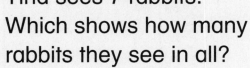

    ⬭   $9 + 7 = 16$

    ⬭   $9 + 2 = 11$

    ⬭   $2 + 7 = 9$

    ⬭   $2 + 5 = 7$

**3.** Draw a picture.
Then complete the
number sentence.

The farm has 4 horses.
It also has 3 pigs.
How many animals does
the farm have in all?

_____ + _____ = _____

Name_____

**1.** Which addition sentence
tells about the picture?

⬭ 3 + 3 = 6

⬭ 4 + 4 = 8

⬭ 5 + 5 = 10

⬭ 6 + 6 = 12

**2.** Kim reads 5 books.
Ralph reads 2 more books
than Kim.
Which addition sentence
shows how many books
Ralph reads?

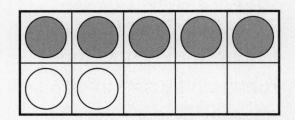

⬭ 1 + 6 = 7

⬭ 5 + 2 = 7

⬭ 3 + 4 = 7

⬭ 0 + 7 = 7

**3.** Write the number sentence for
2 less than 8 is _____.

_____ – _____ = _____

42

Name_____

**1.** Cindy has 10 apples.
She eats 3 apples.
How many apples does
Cindy have left?

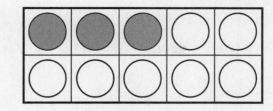

⬭ 3

⬭ 5

⬭ 6

⬭ 7

**2.** Andy has 9 paper clips.
Darleen has 6.
How many more clips
does Andy have?

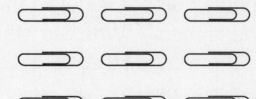

⬭ 9

⬭ 6

⬭ 4

⬭ 3

**3.** Circle the part that repeats.

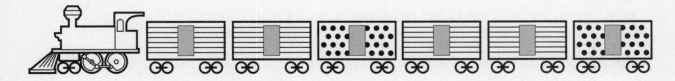

**1.** Find the pattern.
Which letters come next?

- B F Q
- F B Q
- F Q B
- Q B F

**2.** Martha's number is between 5 and 8.
It is less than 7. Which is Martha's number?

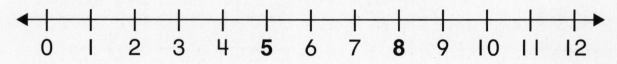

- 4
- 5
- 6
- 7

**3.** Mr. Miles writes this number sentence on the board.

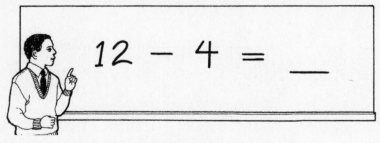

$$12 - 4 = \underline{\quad}$$

Write an addition fact you can
use to find the answer.

_____ + _____ = _____

**44**

**1.** Which letters match the pattern?

⬭ A A B A A B

⬭ A B A B A B

⬭ A B C A B C

⬭ B A B A B A

**2.** The store has 11 hats.
8 hats are sold.
Which addition fact can
help you find how many
hats are left?

⬭ 5 + 3 = 8

⬭ 8 + 3 = 11

⬭ 5 + 6 = 11

⬭ 11 + 8 = 19

**3.** Find the pattern.
Draw what comes next.

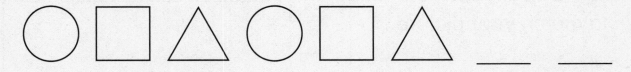

**1.** Which shapes come next in the pattern?

- ☆ ☆
- ☆ ⚾
- ⚾ ☆
- ⚾ ⚾

**2.** Luke and Lucy have 12 pencils in all.
Luke has 5 pencils.
How many pencils does Lucy have?

- 17
- 8
- 7
- 6

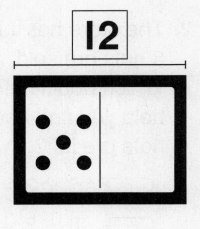

**3.** Draw 1 balloon less than
the number of balloons
in the top box.

Write an addition sentence
and a subtraction sentence
to match your picture.

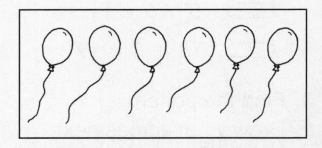

6 + _____ = _____

_____ − _____ = 6

**1.** Cal can put 14 stamps on each page of his stamp book. There are 10 stamps on a page. How many more stamps could fit on the page?

⬭ 1

⬭ 2

⬭ 3

⬭ 4

**2.** Sari uses counters and a ten-frame to show the number of green crayons she has. How many green crayons does Sari have?

⬭ 19

⬭ 15

⬭ 10

⬭ 1

**3.** Write the fact that completes the fact family.

10 + 7 = 17
7 + 10 = 17
17 − 7 = 10

_____ ◯ _____ ◯ _____

**I.** Complete the sentence.
   13 is 10 and _____.

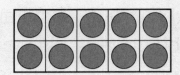

   ⬭ I

   ⬭ 3

   ⬭ 10

   ⬭ 13

**2.** Jay makes 15 paper frogs.
   He gives 4 to his sister.
   How many paper frogs
   does Jay have left?

   ⬭ 19

   ⬭ 15

   ⬭ II

   ⬭ 8

**3.** Gil solved 17 math problems.
   Bonnie solved 2 fewer than Gil.
   How many problems did
   Bonnie solve?

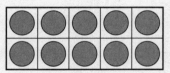

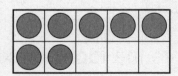

_____ problems

**I.** Sami drew the three cards below.
Which shows the numbers
in order from least to greatest?

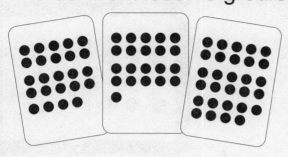

- ⬭ 24, 29, 21
- ⬭ 29, 21 24
- ⬭ 21, 29, 24
- ⬭ 21, 24, 29

**2.** Jason saves 10¢ each day.
He saves his money for 3 days.
How much money does Jason have?

- ⬭ 3¢
- ⬭ 13¢
- ⬭ 15¢
- ⬭ 30¢

**3.** Julie strings beads to make bracelets.
She needs 10 beads for each bracelet.
How many bracelets can Julie make
with 80 beads?

_____ bracelets

Name_____

1. Kali has 11 marbles and 2 bags.
   She put 6 marbles in one bag.
   How many marbles does Kali
   put in the other bag?

    ⬭  9

    ⬭  8

    ⬭  5

    ⬭  3

2. Toni is counting buttons.
   She counts to 86.
   What number will Toni
   say next?

    ⬭  96

    ⬭  87

    ⬭  85

    ⬭  77

3. Write the missing numbers.

| 81 |    |    | 84 | 85 |    | 87 |    | 89 |     |
|----|----|----|----|----|----|----|----|----|-----|
|    | 92 | 93 |    |    | 96 |    | 98 |    | 100 |

**1.** What comes next in the pattern?

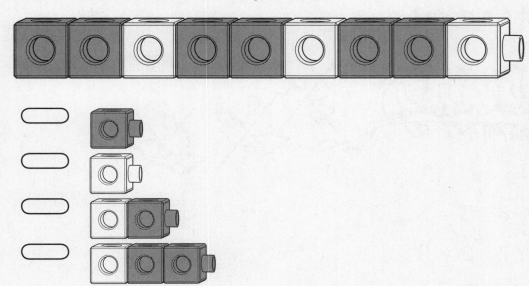

**2.** Selma is counting back by 1s from 75.
What number will Selma say next?

- 76
- 74
- 65
- 64

**3.** Draw counters to solve.
Write the numbers.
Sam has 16 rocks and 2 boxes.
He put 10 rocks in one box.
How many rocks does he put
in the other box?

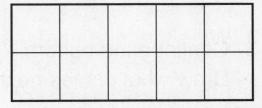

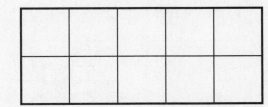

_____ rocks

_____ + _____ = _____

**1.** Which subtraction sentence tells
about the picture?

- $8 - 3 = 5$
- $7 - 3 = 4$
- $8 - 5 = 3$
- $5 - 3 = 2$

**2.** Which number can you make using doubles?

- 3
- 7
- 9
- 12

**3.** Continue the pattern.
Draw what comes next.

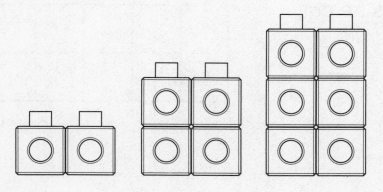

**1.** Which number sentences tell about the model?

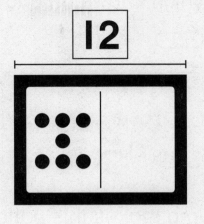

12

$\bigcirc$  $7 + 2 = 9$
$9 - 2 = 7$

$\bigcirc$  $7 + 5 = 12$
$7 - 4 = 3$

$\bigcirc$  $7 + 5 = 12$
$12 - 7 = 5$

$\bigcirc$  $5 + 2 = 7$
$9 + 3 = 12$

**2.** Which is the missing number?

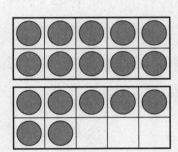

$17 + \underline{\hspace{1cm}} = 20$

$\bigcirc$  1

$\bigcirc$  2

$\bigcirc$  3

$\bigcirc$  5

**3.** Write the numbers you say when you count by 2s.

| 71 | 72 | 73 | 74 | 75 | 76 | 77 | 78 | 79 | 80 |
|----|----|----|----|----|----|----|----|----|----|

_____

**1.** Which shows an odd number?

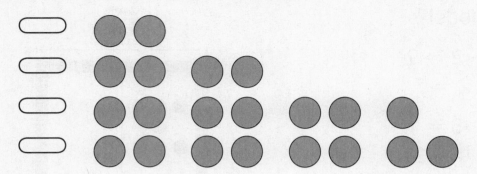

**2.** Uma makes this pattern.

Fran makes the same pattern,
but she uses letters.
What letters come next in
Fran's pattern?

⬭ A A B

⬭ A A A

⬭ B A A

⬭ B B A

**3.** Write the missing number.

13 = 6 + _____

Name_____

Daily TEKS/TAKS
Review **10-1**

**1.** Which shapes come next?

**2.** Each bag has 5 seashells in it. How many seashells are there in all?

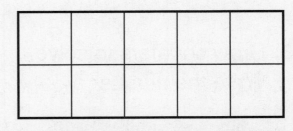

⬭ 30

⬭ 20

⬭ 11

⬭ 6

**3.** There are 15 frogs in the pond. Draw counters to show the number of frogs. Circle **Even** or **Odd**.

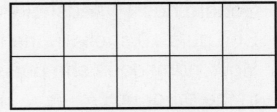

**Even**     **Odd**

© Pearson Education, Inc. 1

55

Name_____

**1.** There are 7 toys.
Each toy has 2 batteries.
Skip count to find how many
batteries in all.

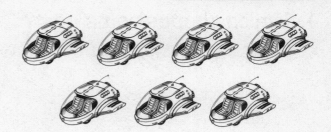

⬭ 14

⬭ 13

⬭ 9

⬭ 5

**2.** There are 5 boats on the lake.
3 more boats join them.
How many boats are on the
lake now?

⬭ 2

⬭ 8

⬭ 9

⬭ 10

**3.** Draw counters to solve.
Write the number.

Sandra has 14 seashells and 2 boxes.
She puts 10 shells in the first box.
How many does she put
in the other box?

_____ seashells

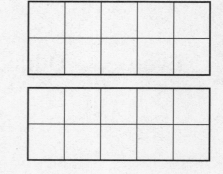

**1.** Find the pattern.
Which comes next?

- ⬭
- ⬭
- ⬭
- ⬭

**2.** Helene has 11 medals.
3 of her medals are gold.
The rest are silver.
Which addition fact could help
you find how many medals are silver?

- ⬭ $3 + 8 = 11$
- ⬭ $3 + 11 = 14$
- ⬭ $11 + 3 = 14$
- ⬭ $11 + 8 = 19$

**3.** Circle groups of 10 fish.
Count how many groups.

_____groups of tens is _____ fish.

**1.** A teacher has 67 crayons.
She wants to make bunches of 10.
How many bunches will she have?

⬭ 7 bunches, with 0 crayons left over

⬭ 7 bunches, with 6 crayons left over

⬭ 6 bunches, with 0 crayons left over

⬭ 6 bunches, with 7 crayons left over

**2.** Gerry sees this pattern.

He makes the same pattern using letters.
Which is his letter pattern?

⬭ A B B   A B B   A B B

⬭ A B A   A B A   A B A

⬭ B B A   B B A   B B A

⬭ A B C   A B C   A B C

**3.** Yuri reads 12 stories.
Joan reads 15 stories.
Kevin reads 13 stories.
Write the numbers in order from least to greatest.

_____   _____   _____
least     between   greatest

Name_____

Daily TEKS/TAKS
Review **11-1**

**1.** Which subtraction sentence
tells about the picture?

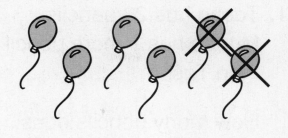

$\bigcirc$    $4 - 4 = 0$

$\bigcirc$    $4 - 2 = 2$

$\bigcirc$    $6 - 4 = 2$

$\bigcirc$    $6 - 2 = 4$

**2.** Which is the missing number?

32 is _____ tens and 2 ones.

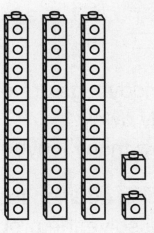

$\bigcirc$    30

$\bigcirc$    10

$\bigcirc$    3

$\bigcirc$    2

**3.** Joyce reads 7 books on Monday.
She reads 2 more on Tuesday.

Write an addition sentence that
tells how many books Joyce reads.

_____ + _____ = _____

© Pearson Education, Inc. 1

**1.** Tasha has 23 pencils.
Marlee has 1 more pencil
than Tasha.

How many pencils does
Marlee have?

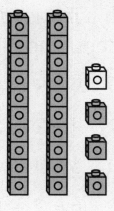

⬭ 25

⬭ 24

⬭ 22

⬭ 4

**2.** 11 ladybugs are on a flower.
4 fly away.
How many ladybugs are left?

Which addition fact can help
you solve the problem?

⬭ 4 + 7 = 11

⬭ 4 + 11 = 15

⬭ 11 + 4 = 15

⬭ 7 + 11 = 18

**3.** Write the missing numbers.

30, 40, _____, _____, 70, _____

**1.** Which number is 10 less than 52?

⬭ 53

⬭ 51

⬭ 42

⬭ 41

**2.** Bill catches a fish.
Lindsey catches a fish.

Which sentence is true?

⬭ Bill's fish is shorter.

⬭ The fish are the
same length.

⬭ Lindsey's fish is longer.

⬭ Bill's fish is longer.

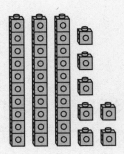

**Lindsey        Bill**

**3.** Write how many cubes.

Write **<**, **>**, or **=** to compare
the numbers.

_____ ◯ _____
  gray       white

**I.** Find the pattern.
Which letter is missing?

   R  B  W  Y  ____  B  W  Y  R

 B

 Y

 R

 W

**2.** Which number makes the sentence true?

14 < _____

⬭ 9

⬭ 10

⬭ 14

⬭ 22

**3.** Write the missing numbers.

| 51 | 52 |    | 54 | 55 | 56 | 57 | 58 | 59 | 60 |
|----|----|----|----|----|----|----|----|----|----|
| 61 | 62 | 63 |    | 65 |    | 67 | 68 |    | 70 |
|    | 72 | 73 | 74 | 75 |    | 77 |    | 79 | 80 |
| 81 |    | 83 | 84 |    | 86 | 87 | 88 | 89 |    |

Name_____

**1.** Henry has more than 25 CDs.
Which could be the number
of CDs Henry has?

⬭ 15

⬭ 19

⬭ 25

⬭ 30

**2.** Which tells how many in all?

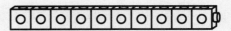

⬭ 10 groups of three
and 3 left over

⬭ 5 groups of tens
and 4 left over

⬭ 4 groups of ten
and 3 left over

⬭ 3 groups of ten
and 4 left over

**3.** Draw lines to show where the numbers go.

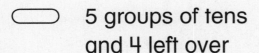

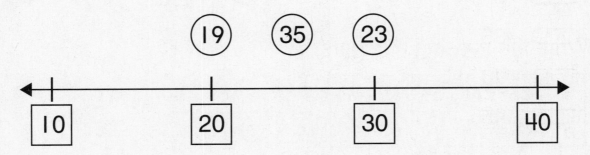

Name_____

**1.** Find the pattern.

Which part repeats?

◯

◯

◯

◯

**2.** Margarita has 8 necklaces. Each necklace has 5 beads.

How many beads are there in all?

◯ 8

◯ 35

◯ 40

◯ 45

**3.** Write the missing number.

_____ is 1 before 80.

**1.** Ann took 27 photographs.
Carl took 10 less than Ann.

| 16 | 17 | 18 | 19 | 20 |
|----|----|----|----|----|
| 26 | 27 | 28 | 29 | 30 |
| 36 | 37 | 38 | 39 | 40 |

How many photographs did
Carl take?

 ⬭ 37

 ⬭ 36

 ⬭ 26

 ⬭ 17

**2.** 4 dogs are playing.
5 dogs join them.

Which number sentence shows
how many dogs in all?

 ⬭ $9 + 5 = 14$

 ⬭ $5 + 4 = 9$

 ⬭ $9 - 5 = 4$

 ⬭ $5 - 4 = 1$

**3.** Nina puts marbles in 3 bags.

Write the numbers in order
from greatest to least.

_____   _____   _____

greatest      least

Name_____

**1.** Which car is fifth?

⬭

⬭

⬭

⬭

**2.** Tang made 38 snowballs.
Eve made 24 snowballs.
Rosa made the fewest snowballs.

Which could be the number
of snowballs Rosa made?

⬭ 19

⬭ 32

⬭ 40

⬭ 45

**3.** Write all the ways to show
24 as tens and ones.

| | |
|---|---|
| | |
| | |
| | |

66

1. Which date is on the second Thursday of April?

| S | M | T | W | T | F | S |
|---|---|---|---|---|---|---|
| 1 | 2 | 3 | 4 | 5 | 6 | 7 |
| 8 | 9 | 10 | 11 | 12 | 13 | 14 |
| 15 | 16 | 17 | 18 | 19 | 20 | 21 |
| 22 | 23 | 24 | 25 | 26 | 27 | 28 |
| 29 | 30 | | | | | |

⬭ 5

⬭ 12

⬭ 20

⬭ 26

2. Which activity takes less time than doing homework?

⬭ Build a dog house.

⬭ Brush teeth.

⬭ Play a game.

⬭ Go shopping.

Use the calendar. Circle **True** or **False**.

3. April has an even number of days.

| April | | | | | | |
|---|---|---|---|---|---|---|
| 1 | 2 | 3 | 4 | 5 | 6 | 7 |
| 8 | 9 | 10 | 11 | 12 | 13 | 14 |
| 15 | 16 | 17 | 18 | 19 | 20 | 21 |
| 22 | 23 | 24 | 25 | 26 | 27 | 28 |
| 29 | 30 | | | | | |

**True**          **False**

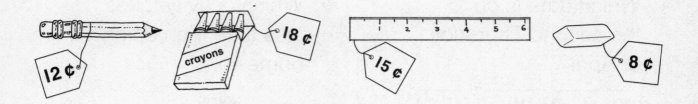

1. Mia wants to buy a box of crayons.
   Which coins could she use?

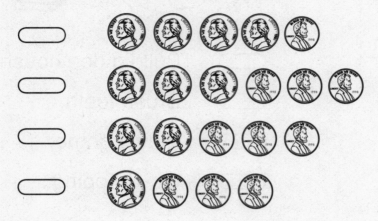

2. How much money does Carlos need
   to buy a pencil and an eraser?

   ⬭  12¢

   ⬭  20¢

   ⬭  27¢

   ⬭  30¢

3. Rico has 2 nickels and 3 pennies.
   Gina has 12 pennies.
   Who has more money?

   _____

**1.** Which coins can Denzel use to buy a glass of lemonade?

**2.** Meg has 1 dime and 4 nickels. How many glasses of lemonade can Meg buy?

    2

    3

    4

    6

**3.** Mia's mother gave her 1 dime, 3 nickels, and 2 pennies. How much more does Mia need to make 30¢?

_____¢

**1.** Alexis has 4 coins.
They are worth 25¢.
Which coins does Alexis have?

**2.** Which coins match the price of the toy giraffe?

**3.** Write the missing number.

5¢        10¢        _____¢        20¢        25¢        30¢

**1.** Gabe has 50¢ in all.
4 coins are nickels.
Which are the other coins?

**2.** Kim has 5 dimes.
Which shows the same amount?

**3.** Write the missing number.

25¢ and _____¢ is 50¢.

Name_____

**1.** How much money in all?

⬭ 66¢

⬭ 69¢

⬭ 74¢

⬭ 79¢

**2.** Zoe sees 14 dragonflies.
Patty sees 4 dragonflies.
How many dragonflies do they see in all?

⬭ 20

⬭ 19

⬭ 18

⬭ 8

**3.** Circle the coins to match the price.

**I.** Which coin has the greatest value?

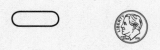

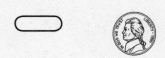

**2.** Marie has 8 flowers.
She gives Bill 3 flowers.
Which shows how many flowers
Marie has left?

   ⬭   $8 - 3 = 5$

   ⬭   $5 + 3 = 8$

   ⬭   $11 - 3 = 8$

   ⬭   $8 + 3 = 11$

**3.** Write $<$, $>$, or $=$ to make the sentence true.

73 ◯ 65

**I.** There are 6 boys and 5 girls
in Ms. Farr's class.
How many children are there in all?

⬭ 7

⬭ 10

⬭ 11

⬭ 12

**2.** Degan has 56¢ in his pocket.
Which coins does Degan have?

⬭

⬭

⬭

⬭

**3.** What number is shown? _____

Name_____

**1.** Dora shaded 1 out of 3 equal parts of a circle.
Which circle did she shade?

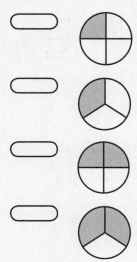

**2.** Ida uses an addition fact to help her solve $8 - 4$.
Which addition fact does she use?

⬭ $2 + 2 = 4$

⬭ $2 + 6 = 8$

⬭ $4 + 4 = 8$

⬭ $8 + 4 = 12$

**3.** Li puts some boxes in a row.
Color the fifth box in the row.

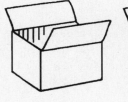 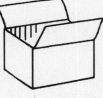   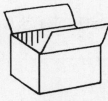

1st        2nd        3rd        4th        5th

**1.** Kenny made a pattern.
He erased one picture in the pattern.
Which picture did he erase?

   ___

 ☆

 ⚾

 ☕

◯ 🥄

**2.** Ms. Grant is 10 years older than Mr. Snow.
Mr. Snow is 27. How old is Ms. Grant?

◯ 73

◯ 37

◯ 28

◯ 17

**3.** Divide the figure into 4 equal parts.
Shade 3 out of the 4 parts.

**I.** Which tells how many
   windows are open?

   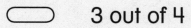   3 out of 4

   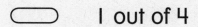   I out of 4

   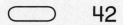   2 out of 3

      I out of 3

**2.** Earl found 34 seashells.
   Roger found 25 seashells.
   Jessica found the most seashells.
   Which could be the number
   of seashells Jessica found?

   ⬭   42

   ⬭   31

   ⬭   29

   ⬭   I9

**3.** Circle the shapes that show equal parts.

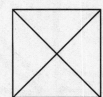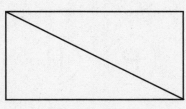

1. Which tells about the bears?

⬭ 2 out of 4 have bows

⬭ 2 out of 6 have bows

⬭ 3 out of 6 have bows

⬭ 4 out of 6 have bows

2. Which doubles fact
does the picture show?

⬭ $2 + 2 = 4$

⬭ $3 + 3 = 6$

⬭ $5 + 5 = 10$

⬭ $6 + 6 = 12$

3. Circle the coins to match the price.

Ⓓ Ⓓ Ⓓ

Ⓝ Ⓝ Ⓝ

Ⓟ Ⓟ Ⓟ

Ⓟ Ⓟ

27¢

**I.** Which racecar is in fourth place?

◯ 15

◯ 21

◯ 23

◯ 36

**2.** Mina gets 9 postcards.
Zack gets 5.
How many more did Mina
get than Zack?

◯ 14

◯ 4

◯ 3

◯ 2

**3.** Lisa and Darnell plant
the same number of flowers.
They plant 18 in all.
Write the doubles fact that
tells about the flowers they planted.

_____ + _____ = 18

1. Paula has 6 CDs.
Bart has 1 more CD than Paula.
Which could you use to find
how many CDs in all?

- ⬭ 2 + 2 and 3 more
- ⬭ 3 + 3 and 1 more
- ⬭ 5 + 5 and 1 more
- ⬭ 6 + 6 and 1 more

2. Which animal is heavier than a cat?

- ⬭ 🐭
- ⬭ 🐦
- ⬭ 🐜
- ⬛ 🐘

3. How much money in all?

___6 4___ ¢

**1.** Which shows equal parts?

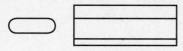

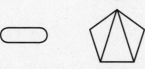

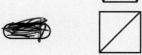

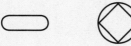

**2.** How much money in all?

⬭ 33¢

⬭ 41¢

⬭ 47¢

⬭̶ 51¢

**3.** Jorge has some marbles.

Fill in the blanks to compare numbers.

_____ ◯ _____
white        black

Name_____

**1.** Joe and Patricia each sold
7 newspapers.
Then Joe sold 2 more.
How many newspapers
did they sell in all?

- ⬭  18
- ⬭  17
- ⬭  16
- ⬭  15

**2.** There are 8 ice cubes. 5 melt.
Which addition fact can help you
find how many ice cubes are left?

- ⬭  2 + 3 = 5
- ⬭  3 + 5 = 8
- ⬭  5 + 8 = 13
- ⬭  8 + 5 = 13

**3.** There are 4 cups.
1 out of 4 is white.
The rest are gray.
Draw the cups.
Write the missing number.

_____ out of 4 cups are gray.

**1.** Pedro and Ann buy the same number of stamps.
They buy 16 stamps in all.
How many stamps did Ann buy?

⬭ 9

⬭ 8

⬭ 7

⬭ 6

**2.** How many equal parts
does the shape have?

⬭ 1

⬭ 2

⬭ 3

⬭ 4

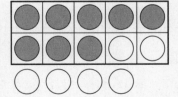

**3.** Jane walked 8 big dogs.
Then she walked 6 small dogs.
Write the missing numbers.

10 + _____ = _____,

so 8 + 6 = _____

Name_____

**1.** How much money in all?

- ⬭ 95¢
- ⬭ 55¢
- ⬭ 50¢
- ⬭ 45¢

**2.** Larry has 9 counters.
Paula has 8 counters.
Which addition fact can help
you find how many counters in all?

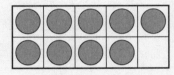
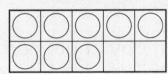

- ⬭ 10 + 6 = 16
- ⬭ 10 + 7 = 17
- ⬭ 10 + 8 = 18
- ⬭ 10 + 9 = 19

**3.** Draw 3 cats.
Circle two thirds of the cats.

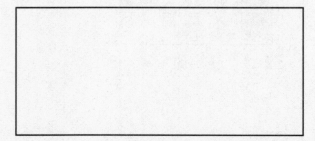

Name_____

**1.** Ellen paints 8 pictures.
Then she paints 9 more.
Which doubles fact can help
you find how many pictures in all?

   ⬭    8 + 8

   ⬭    7 + 7

   ⬭    6 + 6

   ⬭    5 + 5

**2.** 8 dolphins are swimming.
5 more dolphins join them.
Which addition fact can help
you find how many dolphins in all?

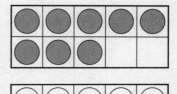

   ⬭    10 + 3 = 13

   ⬭    10 + 4 = 14

   ⬭    10 + 5 = 15

   ⬭    10 + 8 = 18

**3.** Write the numbers.

_____ out of _____ kites have stripes.

**1.** Which is the missing number?

17 = 8 + _____

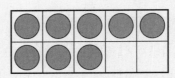

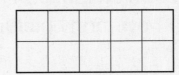

- ⬭  7
- ⬭  8
- ⬭  9
- ⬭  10

**2.** Which is true about the triangles?

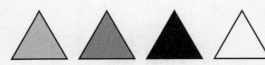

- ⬭  1 out of 3 triangles is white.
- ⬭  2 out of 3 triangles are gray.
- ⬭  1 out of 4 triangles is black.
- ⬭  3 out of 4 triangles are gray.

**3.** There are 7 rooms in the building.
Each room has 10 chairs.
Write the missing numbers.

_____ tens is _____.

There are _____ chairs in all.

1. Mark reads 8 books.
   Ken reads 4 books.
   Which addition sentence
   shows how many books Mark
   and Ken read in all?

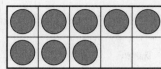

   - $10 + 8 = 18$
   - $8 + 8 = 16$
   - $8 + 4 = 12$
   - $4 + 4 = 8$

2. Allison has 7 new pencils.
   She sharpens 2 of the pencils.
   How many pencils does Allison
   still need to sharpen?

7

   - 2
   - 4
   - 5
   - 9

3. Write an addition sentence for the picture.
   Then write a related subtraction sentence.

   _____ + _____ = _____

   _____ − _____ = _____

**1.** Lupe and Paul have the
same number of keys.
They have 14 keys altogether.
How many keys do they each have?

- ⬭ 9
- ⬭ 8
- ⬭ 7
- ⬭ 6

**2.** There are 8 spiders on a web.
3 crawl away.
Which number sentence shows
how many spiders are left?

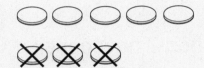

- ⬭ $8 + 3 = 11$
- ⬭ $8 - 3 = 5$
- ⬭ $8 - 5 = 3$
- ⬭ $5 - 3 = 2$

**3.** Oscar wants to buy 2 toys.
He can pick a truck, a robot, or a yo-yo.
Complete the table to show the ways
Oscar can pick the 2 toys.

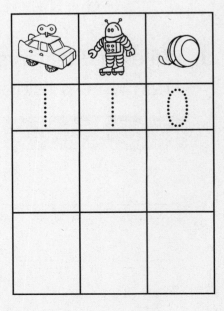

Name_____

**1.** Megan and Albert each have
4 paper clips.
Albert finds 2 more.
How many paper clips
do they have in all?

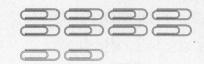

⬭ 8

⬭ 10

⬭ 12

⬭ 14

**2.** Neil has 4 stickers.
Cathy has 2 stickers.
Which number sentence
shows how many stickers they have in all?

⬭ $4 + 6 = 10$

⬭ $6 + 2 = 8$

⬭ $4 + 2 = 6$

⬭ $4 - 2 = 2$

**3.** Write the fact family for the model.

13

_____ + _____ = _____

_____ + _____ = _____

_____ − _____ = _____

_____ − _____ = _____

**1.** Rosa has 7 buttons.
Emma has 4 buttons.
How many more buttons
does Rosa have than Emma?

⬭   3

⬭   4

⬭   5

⬭   11

**2.** There are 11 balloons.
5 balloons pop.
Which addition fact shows
how many balloons are left?

⬭   $11 + 5 = 16$

⬭   $7 + 4 = 11$

⬭   $5 + 6 = 11$

⬭   $11 - 6 = 5$

**3.** First add the circled numbers and
write the sum in the box at the right.
Then write the sum for all 3 numbers.

7

Name_____

**1.** There are 15 ice cubes in a pitcher.
9 ice cubes melt.
Which subtraction fact shows
how many ice cubes are left?

⬭    $9 + 6 = 15$

⬭    $15 - 6 = 9$

⬭    $15 - 9 = 6$

⬭    $9 - 3 = 6$

**2.** There are 2 spiders. Each spider has 8 legs.
Which doubles fact shows how many legs in all?

⬭    $16 = 8 + 8$

⬭    $8 = 4 + 4$

⬭    $12 = 6 + 6$

⬭    $4 = 2 + 2$

**3.** Complete the fact family
for the picture.

$8 + \underline{\hspace{1.2cm}} = \underline{\hspace{1.5cm}}$          $\underline{\hspace{1.5cm}} - \underline{\hspace{1.2cm}} = 8$

$4 + \underline{\hspace{1.2cm}} = \underline{\hspace{1.5cm}}$          $\underline{\hspace{1.5cm}} - \underline{\hspace{1.2cm}} = 4$

1. Paco has 2 pencils.
   Then he buys 3 more pencils.
   Which number sentence shows
   how many pencils in all?

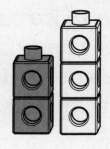

⬭   2 + 1 = 3

⬭   2 + 2 = 4

⬭   2 + 3 = 5

⬭   2 + 4 = 6

2. Arturo has 5 bags.
   Each bag holds 10 marbles.
   Which tells how many marbles
   in all?

⬭   5

⬭   25

⬭   40

⬭   50

3. Sara keeps her books on 3 shelves.
   Each shelf holds 10 books.
   Draw a picture to show how
   many books Sara has.

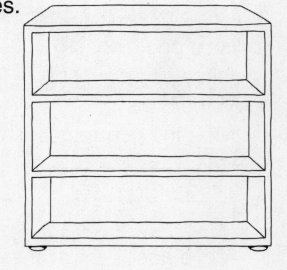

   Sara has _____ books.

**1.** Max has 10 pennies.
Anna has 70 pennies.
How many pennies do Max
and Anna have in all?

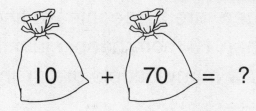

10 + 70 = ?

   ⬭   80

   ⬭   70

   ⬭   60

   ⬭   10

**2.** Look at this part of the hundred chart.
Which numbers complete the pattern?

| 4 |    | 6 |    |
|---|----|---|----|
|   | 15 |   | 17 |

   ⬭   3, 5, 16, 18

   ⬭   5, 7, 14, 16

   ⬭   2, 8, 14, 16

   ⬭   5, 8, 16, 18

**3.** Jaime has 6 bags of hot dog buns.
Each bag holds 10 buns.
Jaime skip counts by 10 to count
all the buns.
Write the numbers Jaime says.

10

_____, _____, _____, _____, _____, _____

Jaime has _____ buns in all.

**1.** There are 57 people waiting in line.
Then 10 more people join the line.
How many people are in line altogether?

   ⬭   67

   ⬭   57

   ⬭   47

   ⬭   10

**2.** Cassie has 34 beads.
Then she buys 10 more beads.
Which shows how many beads in all?

   ⬭   $14 + 10 = 24$

   ⬭   $30 + 10 = 40$

   ⬭   $34 + 10 = 44$

   ⬭   $10 + 44 = 54$

**3.** Matt is counting books.
He has counted to 68.
What are the next 5 numbers he counts?

_____, _____, _____, _____, _____

**1.** Katie has 30 paper clips.
Norman has the same number
of paper clips.
Which shows how many
paper clips in all?

⬭ 30 + 0 = 30

⬭ 30 + 3 = 33

⬭ 30 + 10 = 40

⬭ 30 + 30 = 60

**2.** Alex has 2 groups of stickers.
He has 70 stickers in all.
Which tells about Alex's stickers?

⬭ 50 + 20 = 70

⬭ 70 + 2 = 72

⬭ 50 + 2 = 52

⬭ 25 + 5 = 25

**3.** Follow the clues.
Then write the
addition sentence.

| 41 | 42 | 43 | 44 | 45 | 46 | 47 | 48 | 49 | 50 |
|----|----|----|----|----|----|----|----|----|----|
| 51 | 52 | 53 | 54 | 55 | 56 | 57 | 58 | 59 | 60 |
| 61 | 62 | 63 | 64 | 65 | 66 | 67 | 68 | 69 | 70 |

Start at 42.
Move down 2 rows.
Move right 5 columns.

42 + _____ = _____

**I.** Rosalie has 29 markers.
She buys 3 packages of markers.
Each package holds 10 markers.
Which shows how many markers
Rosalie has now?

29

$\bigcirc$    $29 + 10 = 39$

$\bigcirc$    $29 + 20 = 49$

$\bigcirc$    $29 + 30 = 59$

$\bigcirc$    $29 + 40 = 69$

**2.** Which numbers complete the pattern?

|    | 48 |    |    |
|----|----|----|----|
| 57 |    |    | 60 |

$\bigcirc$    47, 49, 50, 58, 59

$\bigcirc$    67, 47, 46, 58, 59

$\bigcirc$    37, 47, 48, 68, 69

$\bigcirc$    49, 50, 51, 59, 61

**3.** There are 7 flowers in the garden.
Molly picks 4 flowers.
How many flowers are left?
Write a subtraction sentence.

_____ – _____ = _____

**I.** There were 36 apples on the tree.
Jessy picked 10.
How many apples are left on the tree?

⬭ 36

⬭ 26

⬭ 16

⬭ 6

**2.** Sylvia had 58 toys in her closet.
She took out 40 toys.
Which shows how many toys are
left in Sylvia's closet?

⬭ $58 + 40 = 98$

⬭ $58 + 4 = 62$

⬭ $58 - 4 = 54$

⬭ $58 - 40 = 18$

**3.** Follow the clues.
Then write the
addition sentence.

| 71 | 72 | 73 | 74 | 75 | 76 | 77 | 78 | 79 | 80 |
|----|----|----|----|----|----|----|----|----|----|
| 81 | 82 | 83 | 84 | 85 | 86 | 87 | 88 | 89 | 90 |
| 91 | 92 | 93 | 94 | 95 | 96 | 97 | 98 | 99 | 100 |

Start at 75.
Move down 2 rows.
Move right 1 column.

$75 + \rule{2cm}{0.4pt} = \rule{2cm}{0.4pt}$

**1.** Ethan put 29 napkins on the table.
20 napkins were used.
How many napkins are left?

◯ 49

◯ 29

◯ 19

◯ 9

**2.** Danielle had 37 pennies in
her purse.
She gave 12 pennies to Curt.
How many pennies are in
her purse now?

◯ 12

◯ 25

◯ 29

◯ 49

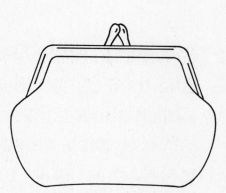

**3.** Follow the clues.
Then write the
subtraction sentence.

Start at 86.
Move up 3 rows.
Move left 2 columns.

| 51 | 52 | 53 | 54 | 55 | 56 | 57 | 58 | 59 | 60 |
|----|----|----|----|----|----|----|----|----|----|
| 61 | 62 | 63 | 64 | 65 | 66 | 67 | 68 | 69 | 70 |
| 71 | 72 | 73 | 74 | 75 | 76 | 77 | 78 | 79 | 80 |
| 81 | 82 | 83 | 84 | 85 | 86 | 87 | 88 | 89 | 90 |

86 − _____ = _____

**1.** There are 78 ants at the picnic.
40 ants leave.
How many ants are still
at the picnic?

⬭ 74

⬭ 48

⬭ 38

⬭ 34

**2.** Jill has 8 CDs.
Cathy has 2 CDs.
Which number sentence
shows how many more CDs
Jill has than Cathy?

⬭ $8 + 2 = 10$

⬭ $10 - 2 = 8$

⬭ $8 - 2 = 6$

⬭ $6 - 2 = 4$

**3.** Use part of the hundred
chart to subtract.

$59 - 32 =$ _____

| 21 | 22 | 23 | 24 | 25 | 26 | 27 | 28 | 29 | 30 |
|----|----|----|----|----|----|----|----|----|----|
| 31 | 32 | 33 | 34 | 35 | 36 | 37 | 38 | 39 | 40 |
| 41 | 42 | 43 | 44 | 45 | 46 | 47 | 48 | 49 | 50 |
| 51 | 52 | 53 | 54 | 55 | 56 | 57 | 58 | 59 | 60 |

**I.** Mimi's puzzle has 48 pieces.
Tiffany's has 56.
Pat's puzzle has more pieces than Mimi's
and fewer pieces than Tiffany's.
Which can be the number of pieces
in Pat's puzzle?

⬭ 46

⬭ 47

⬭ 53

⬭ 58

**2.** A tree has 37 leaves.
20 leaves fall off the tree.
How many leaves are left?

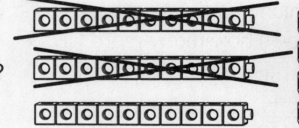

⬭ 35

⬭ 27

⬭ 17

⬭ 15

**3. Complete the model.**
**Then write the missing numbers.**

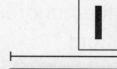

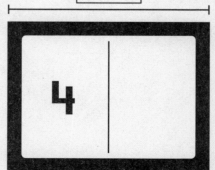

$4 + \underline{\quad} = 11$

$11 - \underline{\quad} = 4$

**1.** Each shirt has 5 buttons.
How many buttons in all?

⬭ 5

⬭ 10

⬭ 20

⬭ 25

**2.** Which shape is a triangle?

⬭ △

⬭ ◻

⬭ ◇

⬭ ○

**3.** Color 2 out of 3 equal parts.

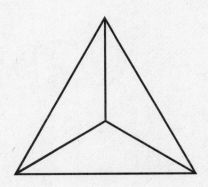

**1.** Brenda draws a shape with 3 sides.
Which shape does she draw?

⬭ square

⬭ circle

⬭ rectangle

⬭ triangle

**2.** How many corners does
this shape have?

⬭ 7

⬭ 6

⬭ 5

⬭ 4

**3.** The pet store sells birds and hamsters.
Bernardo wants to buy 3 pets.
Which ways can Bernardo buy 3 pets?

| Number of birds | 3 | | | |
|---|---|---|---|---|
| Number of hamsters | 0 | | | 3 |

1. Johnny's bag has 50 seeds.
   Brenda's bag has 30 seeds.
   How many seeds do they have in all?

   ⬭ 8

   ⬭ 53

   ⬭ 70

   ⬭ 80

2. There are 13 bats in a cave.
   5 bats fly away.
   Which addition fact can help
   you find how many bats are left?

   ⬭ $5 + 5 = 10$

   ⬭ $8 + 5 = 13$

   ⬭ $5 + 13 = 18$

   ⬭ $8 + 13 = 21$

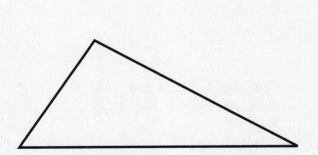

3. Circle the corners.
   Write how many corners.

   There are _____ corners.

Name _____

**1. How much money in all?**

     ⬭   6¢

     ⬭   25¢

     ⬭   30¢

     ⬭   60¢

**2. Which figure is a cone?**

     ⬭   ⬤

     ⬭   △

     ⬭   ◻

     ⬭   ⬭

**3.** Write the numbers in order
from least to greatest.

| 61 | 59 | 68 |
|----|----|----|

_____   _____   _____

  least    between   greatest

**1.** There are 64 mice.
30 are white.
The rest are brown.
How many are brown?

⬭ 94 mice

⬭ 61 mice

⬭ 34 mice

⬭ 31 mice

**2.** Which figure has 8 vertices and
6 flat surfaces?

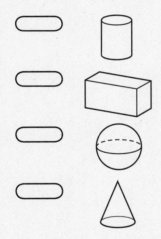

**3.** Sara buys 8 tickets.
Chuck buys 7 more.
How many tickets do
Sara and Chuck have in all?
Draw counters to help you add.
Write the missing numbers.

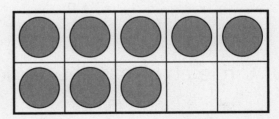

10 + ____ = ____ so, 8 + 7 = ____.

**1.** Anita's necklace has
39 beads.
Jane's necklace has 20.
How many more beads
are on Anita's necklace?

| 11 | 12 | 13 | 14 | 15 | 16 | 17 | 18 | 19 | 20 |
|----|----|----|----|----|----|----|----|----|----|
| 21 | 22 | 23 | 24 | 25 | 26 | 27 | 28 | 29 | 30 |
| 31 | 32 | 33 | 34 | 35 | 36 | 37 | 38 | 39 | 40 |

⬭ 59

⬭ 37

⬭ 19

⬭ 9

**2.** Which shape is a rectangular prism?

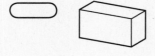

**3.** Circle objects with 0 vertices.

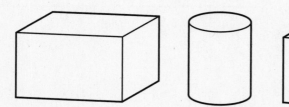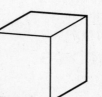

**1.** Andy recycles 59 cans.
Samantha recycles 76 cans.
Tina recycles 67 cans.

Which shows the numbers in order
from greatest to least?

⬭ 59, 67, 76

⬭ 59, 76, 67

⬭ 76, 59, 67

⬭ 76, 67, 59

**2.** Which figure has 0 flat surfaces?

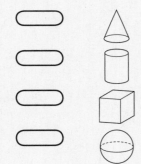

**3.** Use these 3 plane shapes
to make a different shape.
Then draw your new shape.

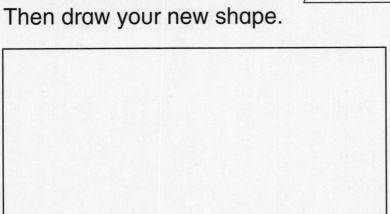

I. Gordon has 43 seeds.
He plants 30 of them.
How many seeds does
Gordon have left?

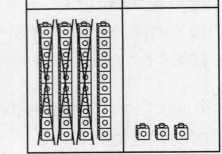

⬭ 10 seeds

⬭ 13 seeds

⬭ 23 seeds

⬭ 33 seeds

2. Which caterpillar is the shortest?

A

B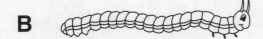

C

D

⬭ A

⬭ B

⬭ C

⬭ D

3. Draw a shape with 6 vertices.

How many straight sides
does your shape have?

_____ sides

108

**1.** How much money in all?

- ⬭ 23¢
- ⬭ 28¢
- ⬭ 58¢
- ⬭ 63¢

**2.** Which is the best estimate
for the length of the sunglasses?

- ⬭ about 10 cubes
- ⬭ about 6 cubes
- ⬭ about 5 cubes
- ⬭ about 3 cubes

**3.** Susan's crayon is shorter
than Ben's crayon.

Draw Susan's crayon.

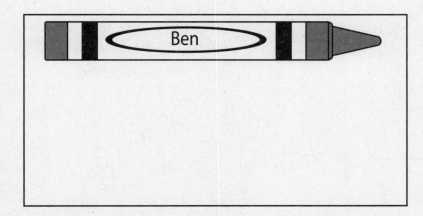

**I.** Which ladder is longest?

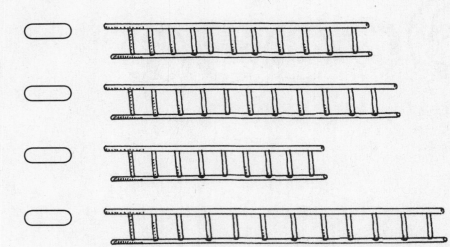

**2.** A baby blanket is about
8 crayons long.
About how many paper clips
long would the blanket be?

about 4 paper clips

about 8 paper clips

about 16 paper clips

about 30 paper clips

**3.** Circle the figure
that has 2 flat surfaces.

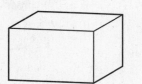

1. Delia makes 8 sandwiches.
Each sandwich has 2 slices of bread.
How many slices of bread in all?

⬭　　8 slices

⬭　　10 slices

⬭　　16 slices

⬭　　18 slices

2. 4 students cover tables with squares.
Whose table has the greatest area?

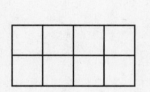 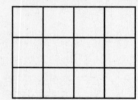 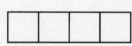 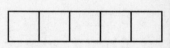

Tanya's table　　Ryan's table　　Alex's table　　Fredric's table

⬭　　Tanya's table

⬭　　Ryan's table

⬭　　Alex's table

⬭　　Fredric's table

3. Write the numbers in order
from least to greatest.

_____  _____  _____

Name_____

**1.** About how long is the comb?

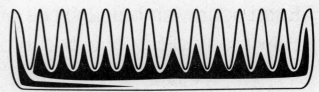

   ⬭    about 12 cubes

   ⬭    about 9 cubes

   ⬭    about 5 cubes

   ⬭    about 3 cubes

**2.** Which container holds the most?

   ⬭

   ⬭

   ⬭

   ⬭

**3.** Circle the rectangle with the smallest area.

**1.** Which would you need the fewest of
to measure the length of a baseball bat?

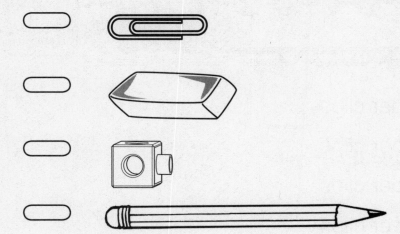

**2.** Which object is lightest?

**3.** Jamie, Oscar, and Nancy each have a glass.
Nancy's glass holds the most.
Draw Nancy's glass.

Oscar                    Jamie                    Nancy

**I.** About how long is the bracelet?

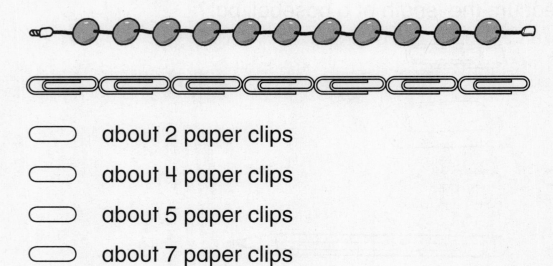

⬭ about 2 paper clips

⬭ about 4 paper clips

⬭ about 5 paper clips

⬭ about 7 paper clips

**2.** Which shows the objects
in order from heaviest to lightest?

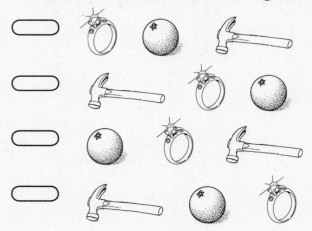

**3.** Circle the picture that shows the coldest weather.

114

**1.** Brad has 7 markers.
He gives 2 to Rita.
How many markers does Brad have left?
Which addition fact can you use to subtract?

⬭   $2 + 2 = 4$

⬭   $2 + 5 = 7$

⬭   $2 + 7 = 9$

⬭   $7 + 2 = 9$

**2.** Which shape shows 2 out of 4 equal parts?

⬭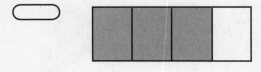

⬭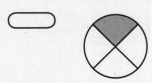

⬭

⬭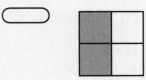

**3.** Circle the picture that shows the coldest temperature.

**1.** Ernest has 12 buckets.
He fills 6 of them with sand.
Which shows how many buckets
do not have sand?

⬭ $12 - 6 = 6$

⬭ $12 - 2 = 10$

⬭ $12 - 9 = 3$

⬭ $12 - 8 = 4$

**2.** When was Sandy talking
on the phone?

⬭ 12 o'clock

⬭ 6 o'clock

⬭ 4 o'clock

⬭ 2 o'clock

**3.** How many △ do you need
to make this shape?

_____

**1.** How many vertices does a circle have?

◯  4 vertices

◯  2 vertices

◯  1 vertex

◯  0 vertices

**2.** How long is the worm?

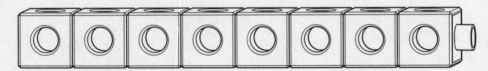

◯  3 cubes

◯  4 cubes

◯  5 cubes

◯  8 cubes

**3.** Draw the clock hands.
Then write the time on the other clock.

7 o'clock

1. A can of soup is the same shape as which solid?

   ⬭   sphere

   ⬭   cylinder

   ⬭   cube

   ⬭   cone

2. Which container holds the least?

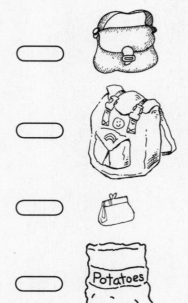

3.

The time shown on the clock is _____ : _____.

**I.** Which time shows when Kyle
wakes up?

- ⬭ 6:00
- ⬭ 6:30
- ⬭ 8:00
- ⬭ 8:30

**2.** Which activity takes the least amount of time?

⬭

⬭

⬭

⬭

**3.** Circle the best tool to find out
how cold a swimming pool is.

Name_____

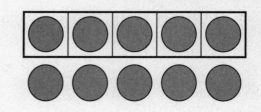

**1.** Jake draws 5 counters.
Then he draws 5 more.
Which number sentence shows
how many counters in all?

 $5 + 10 = 15$

 $5 + 5 = 10$

 $5 + 0 = 5$

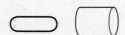 $5 - 5 = 0$

**2.** Which solid figure does not roll?

**3.** Shade 1 out of 2 equal parts of the rectangle.

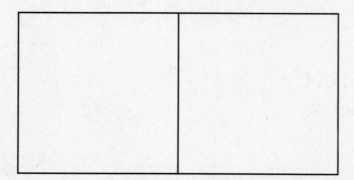

**120**

**1.** Which ball of yarn is longest?

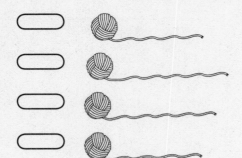

**2.** Which tells a half hour before?

⬭ 4:00

⬭ 3:30

⬭ 3:00

⬭ 2:30

**3.** Write a number sentence for the picture.

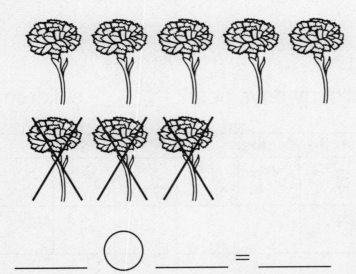

_____ ◯ _____ = _____

**1.** Which tells about the picture?

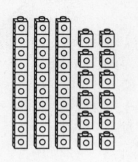

◯    3 tens 12 ones < 4 tens 2 ones

◯    3 tens 12 ones > 4 tens 2 ones

◯    3 tens 12 ones = 4 tens 2 ones

◯    42 ones > 4 tens 2 ones

**2.** Which is the missing number?

73 – _____ = 43

◯    33

◯    30

◯    27

◯    20

**3.** How many children like cloudy days best? _____ children

| Favorite Weather | | | | | | | | |
|---|---|---|---|---|---|---|---|---|
| ☀ Sunny | ☀ | ☀ | ☀ | ☀ | ☀ | ☀ | ☀ | ☀ |
| ⛅ Cloudy | ⛅ | ⛅ | ⛅ | | | | | |
| 🌧 Rainy | 🌧 | | | | | | | |

**1.** Which describes the set?

⬭  1 out of 4 shirts have stripes

⬭  3 out of 4 shirts have stripes

⬭  4 out of 4 shirts have stripes

⬭  2 out of 4 shirts have stripes

**2.** Which describes the pattern?

⬭  A B A

⬭  A B B

⬭  A B C

⬭  A A B

**3.** How many children go to bed at 9:00?

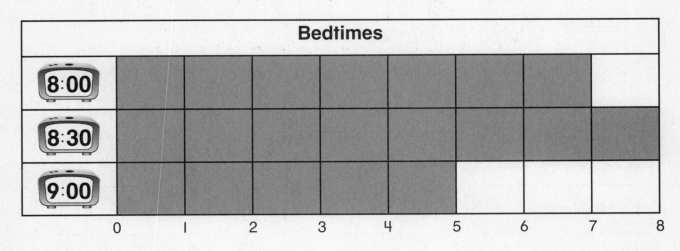

_____ children go to bed at 9:00.

1. Candice uses an addition fact to help her solve 13 − 5.
   Which related addition fact could she use?

   ⬭   5 + 5 = 10

   ⬭   5 + 6 = 11

   ⬭   5 + 7 = 12

   ⬭   5 + 8 = 13

2. Which club has the fewest members?

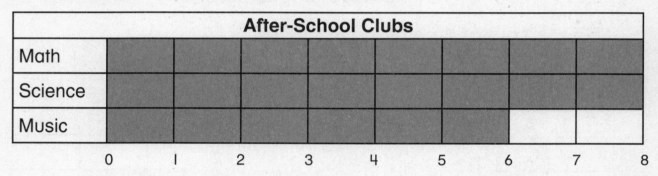

**After-School Clubs**

| | 0 | 1 | 2 | 3 | 4 | 5 | 6 | 7 | 8 |
|---|---|---|---|---|---|---|---|---|---|
| Math | | | | | | | | | |
| Science | | | | | | | | | |
| Music | | | | | | | | | |

   ⬭   Math

   ⬭   Science

   ⬭   Music

   ⬭   Math and Science

3. Color 2 out of 3 parts of the circle.

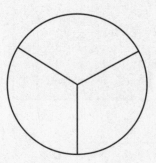

**1.** Which are the missing numbers?

| 82 |    | 84 |    |
|----|----|----|----|
|    | 93 |    | 95 |

⬭  83, 84, 85, 86

⬭  83, 85, 87, 89

⬭  83, 85, 92, 94

⬭  91, 94, 96, 98

**2.** Which is the most favorite color?

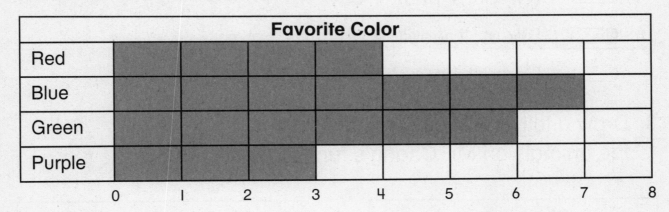

⬭  Red

⬭  Blue

⬭  Green

⬭  Purple

**3.** Write tally marks to show 8.

_____

**I.** Eric has 11 marbles.
He has 8 more marbles than Ken.
How many marbles does Ken have?

⬭ 2

⬭ 3

⬭ 4

⬭ 5

**2.** Which shows the time in order from shortest to longest?

⬭ I hour, I day, I week

⬭ I week, I hour, I day

⬭ I hour, I week, I day

⬭ I day, I hour, I week

**3.** Draw a tally chart for the graph about
the animals on Mr. Chang's farm.

| Mr. Chang's Animals | | | |
|---|---|---|---|
| Cow | ▣ | ▣ | ▣ |
| Chicken | ▢ | ▢ | ▢ | ▢ |

| Mr. Chang's Animals | |
|---|---|
| Cow | |
| Chicken | |

1. Bobby has a pumpkin, an apple,
a banana, and a strawberry.
Which is lightest?

- pumpkin

- apple

- banana

- strawberry

2. Which is the same amount as the coin?

- 1 quarter, 1 dime, 2 nickels

- 1 quarter, 2 dimes

- 1 quarter, 2 dimes, 1 nickel

- 1 quarter, 3 dimes

3. Use the information in the tally chart.
Draw pictures to complete the graph.

| Marta's Marble Collection | |
|---|---|
| ● Black | \|\|\|\| \| |
| ○ White | \|\|\| |

| Marta's Marble Collection | | | | | | |
|---|---|---|---|---|---|---|
| ● Black | | | | | | |
| ○ White | | | | | | |

Name_____

**1.** The number of chairs in a classroom is even.
Which could be the number of chairs?

    ◯ 35

    ◯ 33

    ◯ 30

    ◯ 29

**2.** About how many paper clips long is the spoon?

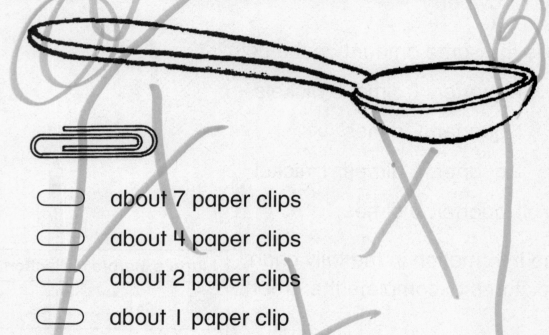

    ◯ about 7 paper clips

    ◯ about 4 paper clips

    ◯ about 2 paper clips

    ◯ about 1 paper clip

**3.** Look at the two groups.
Write a sorting rule that tells how the fish were sorted.

Sorting rule: _____

_____

**1.** Chet makes a tally chart
to show the coins he has.
How many coins does Chet
have in all?

| Chet's Coins | |
|---|---|
| Pennies (P) | 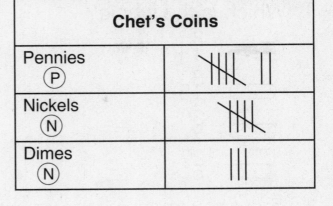 |
| Nickels (N) | |
| Dimes (N) | |

⬭ 18

⬭ 15

⬭ 7

⬭ 5

**2.** Which number is missing from
the related sentences?

_____ $= 17 - 9$

$17 = 9 +$ _____

⬭ 6

⬭ 7

⬭ 8

⬭ 9

17

**3.** Number the objects from lightest to heaviest.
Use **1** for the lightest and **4** for the heaviest.

____  ____  ____  ____

**1.** Which is the whole?

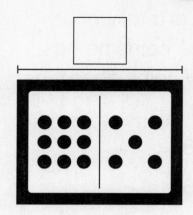

   ⬭   14

   ⬭   13

   ⬭   9

   ⬭   5

**2.** Which part of the fact family is missing?

13 = 8 + 5
13 = 5 + 8
8 = 13 − 5

   ⬭   8 = 18 − 10

   ⬭   5 = 13 − 8

   ⬭   13 = 6 + 7

   ⬭   13 = 10 − 3

**3.** Color the cubes so it is certain
    you will pick a blue cube.

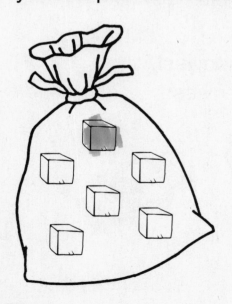